THE COMMEMORATION
OF THE DEAD

THE COMMEMORATION
OF THE DEAD

A STUDY OF
THE ROMANTIC ELEMENT
IN THE "SEPOLCRI" OF
UGO FOSCOLO

An Inaugural Lecture

by

E. R. VINCENT

Fellow of Corpus Christi College;
Professor of Italian in the University
of Cambridge

❋

CAMBRIDGE
AT THE UNIVERSITY PRESS
1936

CAMBRIDGE
UNIVERSITY PRESS

University Printing House, Cambridge CB2 8BS, United Kingdom

Published in the United States of America by Cambridge University Press, New York

Cambridge University Press is part of the University of Cambridge.

It furthers the University's mission by disseminating knowledge in the pursuit of education, learning and research at the highest international levels of excellence.

www.cambridge.org
Information on this title: www.cambridge.org/9781107640238

© Cambridge University Press 1936

First published 1936
Re-issued 2014

A catalogue record for this publication is available from the British Library

ISBN 978-1-107-64023-8 Paperback

THE COMMEMORATION OF
THE DEAD

It is usual for an inaugural address to be one of two kinds, a general survey of the subject concerned or a consideration of some special or typical aspect of it. My three predecessors in this Chair chose the former method, and spoke generally, from their different points of view, of the importance of Italian studies for English people. It is not suitable that I should attempt to say in other words what they have already said so well. I have therefore looked for a subject of sufficient importance to be of some little interest to specialists in the field—even if that interest arises from the opportunity of flatly contradicting my conclusions—and not too detailed or pedantic to distress those of my present audience who have come here today chiefly, perhaps, out of the kindness of their hearts.

The subject of the poem I propose to

consider is a melancholy one, sooner or later of interest to us all, and only too appropriate on this occasion—the commemoration of the dead. Italian studies in general, and Cambridge in particular, have recently suffered heavy losses. Edward Bullough had barely succeeded the late Raffaello Piccoli in this Chair when he was prematurely removed by the hand of death from the position he would have graced so well. Only a few months ago we had to mourn the passing of the Professor Emeritus Thomas Okey, and even since that day another Cambridge man, a beloved leader in our studies, has left us, Edmund Gardner. In the face of these numerous bereavements, which to many of us are personal as well as academic losses, I find it impossible to attempt any kind of formal eulogy, still less an estimation of the considerable contributions to their subject made by these distinguished scholars. It is in the choice of my theme that I can best pay respect to their memory.

The poem *Dei Sepolcri* of Ugo Foscolo

has been recognised as a masterpiece in Italy since its first appearance in 1807, but it is almost unknown in this country. Even amongst those whose literary taste has led them to seek out Dante, Petrarch, Ariosto, and amongst moderns at least Leopardi and Carducci, I find an ignorance of Foscolo unfair to his position in the Italian Parnassus and unfair to his great poetical merit. My hope is that by calling attention to Foscolo today some may be induced to read him. Perhaps this is the most useful function of literary criticism.

My statement as to the neglect of Foscolo in this country is not based only on my own observation. It is significant that, unlike many nineteenth-century Italian poets, he has failed to attract translators. During his stay in England a fragment of the *Sepolcri* translated into English blank-verse appeared in the *European Review*,[1] and there

[1] *European Review*, June, 1824, p. 123. For the whole question of translations of the *Sepolcri v.* G. Calabritto, *The Teacher*, Malta, fasc. 100–102, 1932.

exists in the British Museum the only known copy of another complete translation by an unknown hand, of unknown date. As far as I am aware there was no other until January of 1934, when an English version appeared in the *Bollettino* of the British Institute of Florence.[1] Translators, however, are usually the first to admit that such a poem as the *Sepolcri* can only be appreciated in the original. It is perhaps because a knowledge of Italian was more common amongst literary Englishmen of Foscolo's generation that we lack a complete translation of that time, and in the next generation the interest in Italian letters had unhappily diminished. It is necessary to search for external explanations for the lack of English appreciation of the *Sepolcri* because, despite its *italianità*, there is very

[1] Lorna De' Lucchi, in *Bollettino degli studi inglesi in Italia*, Gennaio, 1934, Firenze. In regard to the translation reported to have been made and destroyed by R. Finch (*v.* Ottolini, *Bibl. fosc.* item 3035) I have found nothing relevant among the Finch MSS. in Bodley.

8

much in the poem to appeal to English taste.

Before attempting any critical observations it will be well to give a résumé of the poem and the ideas it contains, without straying very far from the text.

For Foscolo death is the inscrutable servant of change to be faced courageously without the aid of any transcendental philosophy. Death is deprivation of what we know. All is finished, even hope! Man is swept along through unceasing mutations by an unwearied force of change that soon consigns him and his works and his memorials to oblivion. The opening of the poem describes this desolate fate and Foscolo returns to it again.[1] It would appear that in the face of this inevitable material destruction any attempt to distinguish and commemorate the dead by stone and epitaph is idle. The question underlying the poem, "Should we commemorate the dead?", appears to have

[1] Vv. 95, 231.

found a materialistic negative answer in the first lines. But now begins a magnificent protest against unmeaning annihilation, a protest based on a purely human and historical, rather than a moral, appreciation of the spiritual capacities of mankind. In this consideration we are led far afield from contemporary Milan to renaissance Florence, to England, past the field of Marathon to the plain of Troy. For this reason some criticise the poem as disjointed, but they seem to me to fail in appreciating the inherent unity of thought behind the varying scenes. In the imagination of such a poet the epochs of time meet, and under the scythe of death mankind is one family.

Half musing, the poet gradually moves from the materialism of his exordium. Even if our memorials are to perish, why should we renounce them and thus deny ourselves some brief remembrance on earth. There is a kind of existence, illusory though it may be, in the spiritual bond between the mourner and the mourned:

Celeste è questa
corrispondenza d' amorosi sensi,
celeste dote è negli umani....

The persistence of love beyond death is a gift from Heaven to be cultivated with pious rites, and such rites demand a place to attract and hold the imagination. It is at the grave that we can best perform them. It is the function of the tomb to strengthen the bond of affection between the dead and the living. In fact an abandoned grave and a life without love are implications one of the other.

From these general ideas of wide appeal the poet suddenly turns to an immediate political point. In allusion to certain contemporary decrees he complains that the dead are now to be buried beyond the walls, beyond easy access of the living, and even the commemoration of their names is to be obstructed. He indignantly upbraids Milan for her neglect of the dead body of Parini, whom he reveres above other moderns. All that is gloomy and foul is imagined in order to impress on us the tragedy that the bones of the venerable poet should be for ever lost. The nostalgic mood, the shocked indignation at the fate of the man Foscolo had known and loved, lend a moving personal note to this passage. For a moment it seems as if the poem is to be more of an elegy, but immediately the onward march of thought is resumed.

Ever since man has raised himself above the level of the beasts, his institutions have taught him to respect the remains of the dead. Nature, we know, has destined them for change and dissolution, yet man, as far as he can, strives to protect them. History tells us that tombs have not only been altars of family affection but have also served as national records. They were held to be sacred and were credited with oracular powers. Throughout the ages this religion of tombs has persisted.

What is Foscolo's conception of an ideal place of burial? Not at any rate within a church, for such a custom is not only unhealthy, but grim reminders of death, as such tombs tend to be, depress worshippers and fill the minds of the apprehensive with supernatural fears. The memory of classical rites and his appreciation of what he has heard and read of the rustic English graveyard, paint for the poet the picture of a place of trees and flowers and fountains where mourners find solace and nature lends beauty to love and death. In such a burial place the living may well imagine an intercourse with the dead, especially if a traditional ceremonial gives reality to it.

A scene suddenly presents itself to the poet's imagination and he sees young girls in an English churchyard mourning in charming garden surroundings for their dead mother. For Foscolo, love and patriotism are kindred emotions, and it is not surprising that these English daughters should find it in their hearts in such surroundings to send up a prayer for the hope of their country, the national hero, Nelson. Here, again, the tomb has a two-fold aspect, personal and national. And such it may have in a virile nation—but in Italy? Irony raises its voice. There is indeed no lack of pompous monuments in Italy but they are useless and inappropriate in a country whose national life is base. The ruling classes are entombed already in their own palaces and their boasting crests must serve as epitaph. Yes! the poet's world is dominated by the wealthy and the vile, and he himself can only hope for some tranquil grave at the end, his only legacy a memory of warm affections and of poetry.

But the poem is not to descend to the pathetic, the personal motif is not developed, rather an idea appears that is new, though implicit in what has gone before. The urns of the great are an inspiration to the living. Here for the first time Santa Croce in Florence is consecrated as the Westminster Abbey of Italy. What is it indeed that distinguishes Florence above all other cities? Not only her mild air, her smiling hillsides, her vintage, villas, streams, olives and flowers; not only that she is the mother of poets—of Dante and of Petrarch; not only that she has been richly endowed by nature and art—she is famous because she is the custodian of the great Italians of the past. In Santa Croce lie buried Machiavelli, Michelangelo, Galileo, Alfieri. To these sacred tombs Italians must come to encourage their faith in the destinies of their oppressed country and in the genius of the race.

Here is the climax of the poem. In some fifty lines of sustained eloquence the poet soars in lyrical flight; touching upon the essential qualities of the author of the *Prince* and the builder of St Peter's, he reaches the stars with Galileo, only to stoop and linger lovingly over the idyllic landscape of Tuscany.

What grander variation of theme can there be for an Italian poet, whose blood, let us remember, was half Greek? One only—the tombs of classical antiquity, of

Greece, of Troy. Without apparent effort he takes us from the present back to the remote past. The Italians find inspiration at the tombs of their great dead in Florence; the Greeks were encouraged in their struggle against invaders by the witness of the monuments of their heroes at Marathon.

An army of phantoms rises to fight the battle again. Not, however, by the exercise of their own faculties, for they are dead, and death is, we have already faced the fact, material annihilation. The living human imagination of a passing traveller coasting the shore is necessary to awaken them to action. The fundamental theme of the poem, that of the existence of a communion between dead and living, also underlies this famous passage. It is famous for the use of onomatopœia and alliteration, obvious artifices perhaps, but here introduced with great effect. Wide open words suggest vast, silent, nocturnal space; a metallic clang of hard-ringing consonants breaks in with the din of battle, the clatter of galloping horses spurning the armour of fallen warriors, groans, wailing, battle-hymns, and the song of the Fates.

> *Vedea per l' ampia oscurità scintille*
> *balenar d' elmi e di cozzanti brandi,*
> *fumar le pire igneo vapor, corrusche*
> *d' armi ferree vedea larve guerriere*
> *cercar la pugna; e all' orror de' notturni*
> *silenzi si spandea lungo ne' campi*
> *di falangi un tumulto, e un suon di tube,*
> *e un incalzar di cavalli accorrenti*
> *scalpitanti su gli elmi a' moribondi,*
> *e pianto, ed inni, e delle Parche il canto.*

Once launched upon this classical ocean it is but a short voyage from Greece to Troy. Sailing there, a myth rises to the poet's mind—the contest between Ajax and Ulysses for the arms of Achilles. In life the cunning Ulysses obtained the trophies, but on his death in the waves, the gods bore them on the tide and cast them up on the Trojan beach to lie on the grave of Ajax. Justice can be done to the dead and the grave must be the site of retribution.

Now let the Muses, the true custodians of

tombs, help the poet to his conclusion, for when time shall have relentlessly swept away man's memorials (this hard fact has been faced and admitted), they alone can raise their voices and conquer the dreadful silence. Troy lives for us in poetry.

Dardanus, Assaracus, Ilus, Erichthonius, Priam, Hector—resounding names here give the verse a chanting ritualistic quality as though their repetition gave life to bones long crumbled to nothing. For this too is poetry and therefore has the supreme obligation of immortalising dead heroes.

Jove granted lasting fame to Troy as a boon to his beloved nymph Electra. But the centre of the national life was at the Trojan tombs; there the prophetess Cassandra predicted the great disaster, and there those who returned from Greek bondage were to find the only relics of what had been their city and their nation. May these tombs, Cassandra begs, be revered, and the trees that shelter them respected, for she knows in her prophetic soul that their message is to be heard. From them Poetry is to learn the epic story of Ilium and its fall. An old blind man will grope about the Trojan tombs and finger the urns and question them and, learning all, Homer will immortalise what time would sweep away to limbo. The whole world will hear of the victorious Greeks and mourn the vanquished, and as long as man knows what sorrow is, Hector's tragic fate will be lamented.

> *E tu onore di pianti, Ettore, avrai*
> *ove fia santo e lagrimato il sangue*
> *per la patria versato, e finchè il sole*
> *risplenderà su le sciagure umane.*

Tombs are indeed necessary; all our affections seem to need them and all the most profound sympathies of humanity are bound up in their rites. Love, patriotism and poetry are strong against annihilation, and the tomb itself is the focus of their immortal power.

I hope I shall be excused by the requirements of the present occasion for having given a somewhat lengthy, if most inadequate, description of the poem. I now propose to consider it from a more critical point of view. From the very year of its appearance the *Sepolcri* has been the object of criticism, at first unduly concerned with attributing a category, with attaching the label of sermon, ode, epistle, elegy, satire or epic, to a poem which apparently shared the peculiarities of them all; latterly more occupied in analysing its various elements and studying it in relation to the literary environment of its time. A favourite field for enquiry has been the extent of so-called classical and romantic feeling in the poem. I shall not be tempted to define the words classicism and romanticism, particularly in front of this learned audience, but it is notorious that they are much abused terms. I certainly have always been taught by that shrewd critic, my friend and master, Professor Cesare Foligno of Oxford, that they are not touchstones to be applied to literature as scientists use litmus paper. If such

a test be applied to the *Sepolcri* your re-
agent will be found to be neither red nor
blue, but variegated as a rainbow. W. P.
Ker has a suggestive essay on the subject
of this misused terminology in which he
takes delight in pointing out the romanticism in such poets as Pindar. "Some authors
wish to divide all literature and art between
these two parties. If you are not classical,
you must be romantic; there is no third
party for you to join. If you try to form
a school of your own, you will be told that
this very effort at independence is itself
pure romanticism."[1] Foscolo himself was
not in the least concerned in seeing his
poem allotted to such categories; he described it as "*Poesia lirica*" aiming at the
"*sublime*", and he further said: "I have
derived this method of poetry from the
Greeks." This statement, together with the
classical vocabulary and form, the allusions
to antiquity and the underlying sense of

[1] W. P. Ker, *Collected Essays*, Macmillan, 1925,
p. 331.

fate, has made it easy for critics to label the *Sepolcri* a classical poem containing some romantic elements which they are inclined to limit to certain passages and attribute to specific literary influences. Some, such as Guido Muoni,[1] have stressed the romantic influence of foreign, and particularly English, sepulchral poets; others, such as T. L. Rizzo,[2] have denied this and insisted that the poem is in a purely native tradition even where it is least classical. Cian[3] and Zumbini[4] have indicated interesting parallels with poems of Gabriel Legouvé and notably with Delille's *Imagination*, where tombs are treated as a source of inspiration to the living, and from a social rather than a moral point of view. Where even certain

[1] G. Muoni, *Poesia notturna preromantica*, Milano, 1908; see also E. Bertana, *Arcadia lugubre* in *In Arcadia*, Napoli, 1909.

[2] T. L. Rizzo, *La poesia sepolcrale in Italia*, Napoli, 1927.

[3] V. Cian, *Per la storia del sentimento ecc.*, *Giornale Storico*, xx, 1892, p. 205.

[4] B. Zumbini, *La poesia sepolcrale ecc.* in *Studi di lett. ital.* Firenze, 1906.

of these distinguished critics have touched on romantic feeling and influence in the *Sepolcri* they seem to have been unduly concerned with particular passages and particular authors. It is perfectly true that Foscolo read and admired Gray's *Elegy*, and that a few lines may be echoed in the *Sepolcri*, but it is equally true, as Foscolo himself protested, that the whole feeling and scope of the two works are different. Thomas Parnell in his *Night Piece on Death* has these lines:

> Why then thy flowing sable stoles,
> Deep pendant cypress, mourning poles,
> Loose scarfs to fall athwart thy weeds,
> Long palls, drawn hearses, cover'd steeds,
> And plumes of black, that, as they tread,
> Nod o'er the scutcheons of the dead?
> Nor can the parted body know
> Nor wants the soul, these forms of woe.

This is somewhat similar to the opening of the *Sepolcri*, but Parnell's object is to illustrate the Christian hope of resurrection. So it is in that "wilderness of thought" as Dr Johnson defined the *Night Thoughts* of

Young, so it is with Hervey's *Meditations among the Tombs*, so it is with Robert Blair's *Grave*; these clergymen, for every one of them is a clergyman, are concerned to draw a moral from the tomb precisely as if they were still in the pulpit. They meditate on the vanity, where Foscolo stresses the value, of human achievement. They retire into solitude, Foscolo surrounds himself with all the generations of mankind. They prefer the gloom of night, Foscolo the open scene of day. They seem to find a morbid enjoyment in the decay and dissolution which Foscolo resents and combats with all his vigorous sanity. Young and Hervey, despite their Christianity, appear to be circumscribed by the material, while Foscolo, without it, is free in a spiritual world of his own creation.

It seems an unprofitable occupation to collate passages from authors so fundamentally unlike Foscolo, even where similar passages exist. But by denying any great importance to such comparisons I am far from denying the warm modern sentiment which is so obviously the pulse of the *Sepolcri*, and which places it in that general current of European pre-romanticism which we associate with the names of Young, "Ossian", Rousseau, Gessner and their like. It is significant that a primitive poet, Homer of the Iliad, is the ancient author whose influence is most strongly felt in this poem, certainly far more than that of Virgil.[1] As he appears in the *Sepolcri* Homer has more than a little of an Ossianic bard about him. He gropes his way through a grove of ancient trees, ponders on tombs, sounds his lyre to win an eternity of tears for a fallen warrior. The nocturnal battle of phantoms at Marathon, behind its classical vocabulary, is to me reminiscent of Ossian, and when we find the emphasis in the Trojan scene on the women rather than the heroes, Electra with her *dolci vigilie*, Cassandra appealing to a grove of trees to shelter her

[1] Cf. G. Patroni, *La poesia e la figura d' Omero nei "Sepolcri" del Foscolo*, in *Studi su Ugo Foscolo*, Torino, 1927.

25

dead, and finally when we recognise the *Weltschmerz* behind the eternity of human suffering of the last line, we are forced to the conclusion that if this is classicism it is a classicism *sui generis*.

To illustrate the quality, the romantic quality (if we must use that term), of the *Sepolcri* there are other methods possible for us besides making what I believe to be false analogies with Young and similar sepulchral poets. I wish now to consider the poem from certain aspects not, I believe, previously studied.

The first concerns the connexion between the *Sepolcri* and contemporary books of travel describing Greece and Asia Minor. It is at the account of Marathon in the poem that we first meet a traveller coasting the shore and observing the plain:

Il navigante
che veleggiò quel mar sotto l' Eubea.

Immediately after we find another, Pindemonte, sailing beyond the Aegean islands to Troy:

Felice te che il regno ampio de' venti,
Ippolito, a' tuoi verdi anni correvi!

The Trojan tombs are seen through the eyes
of modern visitors:

Ed oggi nella Troade inseminata
eterno splende a' peregrini un loco;

and in a note to this passage Foscolo calls
our attention to the discoveries of recent
travellers. Now it is exceedingly instructive
to read the books of travel mentioned here
and elsewhere by Foscolo, particularly the
Voyage dans la Troade by Lechevalier and
the *Voyage dans l'Empire ottoman, l'Égypte
et la Perse* of Olivier.[1] Both these travellers
visit Marathon and discuss, one the phan-
tom battle on the evidence of Pausanias,

[1] In a note to *Sepolcri*, vv. 235, 236, edit. Guidotti,
Lucca, 1844, p. 18, referring to the discovery of the
tomb of Ilus, Foscolo mentions *Notizie d' un Viaggio
a Constantinopoli dell' Ambasciadore inglese Liston di
Mr Hawkins, e del Dr Dallaway*. Neither in the
contributions of Hawkins to Walpole's *Miscellanies*,
nor in Dallaway's *Constantinople Ancient and Modern
etc.* 1797, is there anything to warrant this note. I have
failed to find any publication by either of these authors
in book or periodical form to explain the reference.

27

the other the surviving fragments of memorials. Both pass *oltre l' isole egèe* to Asia Minor, and thus incidentally provide a simple explanation for the unexpected change of scene in the poem from Marathon to Troy. Both bring a wholly romantic sympathy to bear on the barrows of the plain of Troy, which they are quite satisfied can be recognised as the burial places of the Homeric heroes. The Iliad comes to life for them as they stand by the side of the tumuli and regard them with awe and affection. It is significant to notice that both Lechevalier and Olivier echo the contemporary interest in methods of burial. The former, for example, writes as follows: "Most ancient peoples placed tombs outside towns and oriental nations still religiously keep to this custom, but the Lacedemonians crowd the dead and the living together within their walls with the same barbarity as ourselves."[1] Olivier has a long passage describing the cemeteries of Scutari in which

[1] J. B. Lechevalier, *op. cit.* 1802, p. 286, trans.

he gives full play to the prevalent sensibility of the day. He tells us of the beauty of those tree-shaded places and of his emotion at seeing a young widow weeping over her husband's tomb. For years after burial of their dear ones mourners come to tend the flowers and trees, to commune with the dead and offer prayers.[1] Now Foscolo knew his Homer intimately and had even translated the Iliad, but he had not been to Troy, and in considering the Trojan section of the *Sepolcri* it is by no means unimportant to realise that he took information from and in some part caught the mood of these modern travellers steeped in the romantic attitude towards tombs. It helps us to realise why the tomb of Ilus is as actual as that of Alfieri in the poem.

There is another approach to the *Sepolcri*, also beyond the limits of purely literary comparison, particularly interesting to an Englishman, as it associates the poem with his own country. One of the symptoms of

[1] G. A. Olivier, *op. cit.* an. IX, Tome I, pp. 42, 43.

the changing taste during the eighteenth century in England, and later abroad, was the new gardening. Under the guidance of such men as Vanbrugh and William Kent the old formal garden gave way to winding walks and carefully natural plantations. Nature was no longer to be restrained by art; art in this case was to be nature. The method was described in books, and the books were read abroad, where the so-called English garden became fashionable. In this way an appreciation of the luxuriant vegetation of the English countryside became more frequent amongst cultivated foreigners. A sympathetic, sometimes sentimental, feeling for trees and flowers grew up and often found literary expression. One of the important works on the new method of gardening was written by the German Hirschfeld, a book which, particularly in French translation as *La Théorie de l'art des Jardins*,[1] had a European circulation.

[1] C. C. L. Hirschfeld, *La Théorie de l'art des Jardins*, Amsterdam, 1779–1785.

In Italy it was plagiarised by a certain Count Ercole Silva, who produced anonymously in 1801 his *Dell' Arte dei Giardini Inglesi*.[1] This book was read by Foscolo, and it is not impossible that he also read Hirschfeld. In any case he was well aware of the aesthetic implications of the new attitude towards gardens owing to his friendship with Ippolito Pindemonte. In 1797 the latter had read a paper on the subject to the Accademia di Scienze, Lettere ed Arti of Padova, in which he proved himself an enthusiastic admirer of the more melancholy charm of the romantic garden, and claimed the honour of its discovery for Italy on the strength of eight lines of Tasso. (He did not mention the landscapes of Salvator Rosa, which would have been possibly more to his purpose!)

With these facts in mind let us now return to the *Sepolcri*. The poem begins with the words *All' ombra de' cipressi*; a few lines farther Foscolo stresses the deprivation of

[1] *Dell' Arte dei Giardini Inglesi*, Milano, Anno IX.

the beauties of nature as one of the first
and most obvious results of death:

> *Ove più il sole*
> *per me alla terra non fecondi questa*
> *bella d' erbe famiglia....*

Following this indication we discover that
trees and flowers play a curiously prominent
part in the poem. It seems that Foscolo
can hardly conceive a tomb without pro-
tective foliage and scented blossoms:

> *e di fiori odorata arbore amica*
> *le ceneri di molli ombre consoli,*

unless it be abandoned and then in contrast
it is left to the nettles. He sits pensive in
a grove (v. 64) regarding the lime tree under
which Parini used to rest, and he imagines
that its fronds hang swaying in dejection
since it cannot offer shade and shelter to
the dead poet as it once did when he lived:

> *sotto quel tiglio*
> *ch' or con dimesse frondi va fremendo,*
> *perchè non copre, o Dea, l' urna del vecchio*
> *cui già di calma era cortese e d' ombre.*

How sad is the lot of the forgotten dead,
a grave where no flower grows:

> *Ah! su gli estinti*
> *non sorge fiore, ove non sia d' umane*
> *lodi onorato e d' amoroso pianto.*

The ideal place of burial is beneath cypresses and cedars that scent the air and, evergreen, symbolise unfading memory:

> *Ma cipressi e cedri,*
> *di puri effluvî i zefiri impregnando,*
> *perenne verde protendean su l' urne*
> *per memoria perenne,....*

Fountains nourish amaranth and violet (vv. 124–126), the heavenly fragrance of flowers consoles mourners (vv. 128, 129). Thus English garden cemeteries form an Elysian background to those who weep for their dead:

> *Pietosa insania che fa cari gli orti*
> *de' suburbani avelli alle britanne*
> *vergini,....*

Florence is described with her hills covered with vines and olives and perfumed with thousands of flowers (vv. 170–172). Even Troy has its trees watered by the tears of widows. Cassandra begs them to shelter the urns of her people as she foresees the day when the blind poet will grope beneath their *antichissime ombre* to find the Trojan tombs (vv. 272–283). This conception of the combination of garden with cemetery is something not only new in Italian poetry, but without example in the coldly formal or neglected burial places of contemporary Italy. Classical poetry and classical tombs are not without their flowers and garlands:

manibus date lilia plenis
purpureos spargam flores...;

but in the *Sepolcri* trees and flowers are not treated as mere embellishments, symbolically or mythologically, they take on a romantic personality which enables them to enter into human sorrows and even desire to alleviate them.

The part played by Ercole Silva's book on garden aesthetics in encouraging Foscolo's modern attitude towards nature is so considerable that I would venture to describe it as a source of ideas no less important than, for example, the poetry of Delille. It is surprising, therefore, that critics

34

appear to have disregarded it.[1] This influence on the *Sepolcri* is by no means restricted to the emphasis on trees and flowers we have just indicated. A prominent place in the new garden was often allotted to memorials, busts or urns, while their effect on the visitor was closely considered. Both Hirschfeld and Silva devote a chapter to the subject. We find reference in the latter to Roman rites and the national importance of preserving the names of great men. He demands distinction of tombs so that those who have deserved well of their country shall not be confused with common citizens. Both authors treat of actual cemetery gardens and the need for diminishing the horror of death by the natural beauty of the surroundings. Hirschfeld incidentally describes the beauty of the Tuscan hills

[1] Partial and incidental reference to Silva's book is made by the following critics: Severino Ferrari, *Liriche scelte di Ugo Foscolo*, Sansoni, 1891; Vittorio Cian, *Per la storia del sentimento e della poesia sepolcrale in Italia ed in Francia ecc.*, *Giornale Storico*, xx, 1892.

much in the way Foscolo does.[1] The fact
that Silva strongly urges the superiority of
burial in rustic surroundings, necessarily
beyond the walls of cities, undoubtedly
influenced Foscolo to such an extent that
we notice contradictory views on this point
in the poem. His resentment against the
Napoleonic decrees which forbade city
burial (vv. 51–53) was forgotten in his
appreciation of Silva's point of view and
the emphasis he gives to garden burial
(vv. 114–118, 130–132).

Particular passages in *Dell' Arte dei Giardini Inglesi* are of special interest to students
of the *Sepolcri*, but, not wishing to strain
your patience, they may well be confined to
a footnote.[2] A single glance, however, at

[1] Having no direct evidence that Foscolo read
Hirschfeld's book, I give this particular reference for
what it may be worth. For Foscolo's knowledge of
Silva, see his note to *Sepolcri*, vv. 130–133, *edit.
cit.*

[2] Quotations from Silva, *op. cit.*, for comparison
with *Sepolcri*: "Tale tributo reso al vero merito,
onora quello, cui è dato, e chi lo discerne; ritiene viva

the engravings illustrating these works on

ne' petti cittadini la memoria dei fasti, e de' progressi
nazionali..." (p. 260).

"Per conservare l' antico rito si costumava pian-
tarvi intorno de' boschi e questi boschi erano riputati
sacri" (p. 215).

"I cimiterj sono que' luoghi, che per loro stessi,
ricordando all' uomo il più luttuoso di tutt' i momenti,
abbisogna che nel loro aspetto diminuiscano il ribrezzo,
che viene causato dall' idea della dissoluzione,
ornandoli con maestosa semplicità di tutti quegli
oggetti, che possono sussidiare l' immaginazione colle
idee del riposo, e della riproduzione. Le piante, che
hanno il verde perenne, come i pini, i cipressi, i tassi,
ed i lauri, sembrano essere esclusivamente volute per
ornare questi ricinti, sia per l' idea funerea, che la
consuetudine vi ha applicata, sia perchè mostrando
queste piante di avere una vitalità permanente, che
non riceve insulto dal verno, consolano l' umana
ambizione, che tanto spesso ama di pascersi di felici
illusioni" (p. 326).

"I loro tumuli [cioè dei Romani] che non nasconde-
vano in angoli remoti, ed oscuri, ma che collocavano in
siti scoperti, e vistosi, e lungo le pubbliche vie" (p. 327).

"Fede ne facciano i colombarj Romani, che ne' vasi
cinerarj ci hanno serbate le memorie di tanti illustri
cittadini colle ceneri unite alle sepolcrali inscrizioni
in piccoli spazj appunto, o nicchie, come i colombi
sogliono praticare per riporre i loro nidi" (p. 329).

"Gli alberi piantati ne' cimiterj non solamente

garden aesthetics is sufficient to show their

servono ad indicare i siti, ove giacciono amate spoglie, ma ancora a purificare l'aria; poichè le piante diminuiscono le cattive esalazioni, o almeno le rendono men perniciose. Gli alberi servono ancora ad arrestare lo stanco passeggiero là dove tanti monumenti atti a commuoverlo gli richiamano in mente interessanti rimembranze, e gli destano utili riflessioni" (p. 327).

"Vi sono de' grossi borghi, e delle piccole città in Inghilterra, dove precisamente i campi santi offrono il solo passeggio pubblico alla popolazione; ma per quanti ornamenti, e quanta delizia vi sia sparsa, non è mai possibile di allontanare totalmente da quelli l'idea della tristezza, e del dolore" (this quoted inaccurately by Foscolo in note to *Sepolcri*, v. 130) (p. 327).

"Li [i cimiterj] frequenta ora il pensatore malinconico, ora le madri piangenti, ora la vedova sposa, e l'orfano figlio, e sentono mitigare per la semplicità degli abbellimenti di quel recinto il dolore, che vengono ad esalare sulle tombe de' congiunti, e degli amici" (p. 328).

"Lodevole è quella legislazione, la quale avendo in cura gli oggetti sovraccennati, ha tenuto di mira di allontanare questi luoghi dall'abitato..." (p. 328).

"La più esatta eguaglianza morale e politica diviene ineguaglianza di fatto; e per conseguenza il sarcofago, che eterna la memoria del liberatore della patria, e del sommo legislatore, sarà più eminente,

38

importance in our present consideration.[1]
Here we see pictures of actual memorials, as
of the famous island tomb of Rousseau,
and imaginary scenes where neo-classical
urns are depicted under the shadow of
sympathetic trees which droop long bran-
e più ornato dell' urna d' un cittadino privato. I padri
additeranno ai figli la storia delle gesta degli avi,
e lodevole invidia, e grata rimembranza faranno
emulare la celebrità dei predecessori" (p. 330).

"Abbiano i cimiterj un sito esposto ai venti, che
purificano l' aria; il paese all' intorno sia solitario,
serio, e tranquillo. Felice chi potendo edificare questi
ricinti in luogo, ove scorrano acque, saprà trarne
il convenevole partito, e introdurrà dei ruscelli
lustrali, che lambendo l' erba, e il piede delle piante
possano contribuire col grato loro rumore ad inter-
rompere il silenzio del luogo" (p. 330).

"Tutte le popolazioni hanno molto contribuito alla
memoria dei loro. I monumenti, che ci rimangono,
ne fanno fede; e le memorie, che ci sono state tra-
mandate dei riti sacri dell' antichità, ci attestano
quanto rispetto s' avesse pei funerali, e pei sepolcri"
(p. 331).

It is to be remarked that in the second edition of
this book published in 1813 Silva inserted several
ideas and phrases taken directly from the *Sepolcri*.

[1] See Silva, *op. cit.* pp. 82, 190, 326, but particularly
Hirschfeld, *passim*.

ches above them as if striving to express a human affection. We see solitary philosophers meditating by the side of urns and startled travellers regarding woodland memorials. The dead and the living are in constant communion while nature spreads a kindly veil about them. Through this *corrispondenza d' amorosi sensi* the generations are bound together, those who have gone communicate their lesson to those who come after, the tomb itself is the altar of a religion both sentimental and social. This is the very essence of the *Sepolcri*.

There is one somewhat curious passage in the *Sepolcri* particularly striking to an English reader. British maidens are described as mourning for their mother in the tranquil surroundings of a churchyard where they had prayed for the safe return of Nelson, the hero who made a coffin from the mast of a captured ship (vv. 130–136). The remarks of commentators[1] have never

[1] The arguments of Pietro Verrua intended to support a completely unorthodox understanding of

40

satisfied my curiosity as to why Nelson is so unexpectedly introduced, and why his coffin is mentioned, and it was not until I studied the English periodicals of the time that I began to have some understanding of the association of ideas in Foscolo's mind. Nelson died on October 21st, 1805, but it was not till January 9th of the following year that he was buried in St Paul's with almost regal pomp. The whole nation had been most profoundly moved by the death of the hero in the hour of victory. The press was filled with panegyrics whose constant theme was the immortality of the hero in the grateful remembrance of his countrymen. His tomb was to be an incentive to patriotism. In view of Foscolo's mention of *britanne vergini* in association with Nelson it is not uninteresting to find that many of these poems were written by ladies. A certain Eliza expresses two of the

the passage seem to me unconvincing. Pietro Verrua, *Orazio Nelson nel pensiero e nell' arte del Foscolo e del Canova*, Padova, 1919.

chief motifs of such poetry in *The Gentle-man's Magazine*:

> Oh! Mourn! through all thy realms
> Britannia, mourn!
> Bind thy sad wreaths around his honoured
> name!
> Yet whilst they bathe with tears their Nelson's
> urn,
> Teach thy brave sons to emulate his fame.[1]

Another lady who signs herself *Une Villa-geoise* gives vent to her feelings in a poem describing the nine muses weeping over Nelson's corpse.[2] The funeral itself was naturally described at length, and the following detail was invariably given: "The inner coffin (lined with lead) was made in the gallant Admiral's life-time from the mast of the *Orient*; and the following attestation is engraved on a large brass plate screwed on the lid: Swiftsure, May 23, 1799. I do certify that every part of this coffin is made of the wood and iron of

[1] *The Gentleman's Magazine*, January, 1806.
[2] *Ibid.* March, 1806.

l'Orient's mast, etc."[1] This, too, was seized on by the amateur poets and we find *Nauticus* writing as follows:

> The splendours of proud Gaul are past!
> Britannia mourns her Nelson's fall.
> E'en foes shall deck his grave—Their mast
> His coffin, and their flags his pall.[2]

I am not, of course, suggesting that these effusions were read by Foscolo; I quote them to show the kind of topics current amongst English people in the early months of 1806. Now precisely at this time Foscolo was at Boulogne attached to the Napoleonic army marshalled there for the invasion of our shores. He was engrossed in the study of English and was much in the company of English ladies living in that part of France. Even if we rule out for these months any influence from the unfortunate Miss Hamilton of Valenciennes, there still remains a certain Miss White, *little enemy* as he called her, with whom he was on sentimental

[1] *Ibid.* January, 1806.
[2] *Ibid.* November, 1805.

terms. It seems highly probable that through such intermediaries the poet caught the spirit of our countrymen in regard to Nelson, and for this reason introduced his name together with *britanne vergini* in his poem on death and burial.[1] The reference is obscure, and perhaps even unfortunate, because he has omitted what one suspects is the real reason for its presence, namely the inspiration to be drawn from a hero's tomb. This idea, however, is developed in the Santa Croce passage, where the tombs of great Italians of the past are considered, and the church of Santa Croce is elevated to the position it had never previously held in Italian tradition, that of a national Valhalla. Such a matter is not susceptible to proof, but I myself am inclined to associate the tomb of Nelson in St Paul's

[1] I do not, of course, insist that Foscolo could only have learned the details of the funeral from his English friends, for it was reported in the French and Italian press. Cf. *Giornale Italiano*, No. 188, 10 Dicembre, 1805, p. 1029, for the coffin made from the mast.

and the feeling his burial aroused in England with the *urne de' forti* in Santa Croce.[1]

In regard to this particular passage, I should like to return for one moment to the question of the neglect of the *Sepolcri* in England in order to point out one echo at least in English poetry. In the fourth canto of *Childe Harold's Pilgrimage* Byron has the following stanza (LIV):

In Santa Croce's holy precincts lie
Ashes which make it holier, dust which is
Even in itself an immortality,
Though there were nothing save the past, and this
The particle of those sublimities
Which have relapsed to chaos: here repose
Angelo's, Alfieri's bones, and his,
The starry Galileo, with his woes;
Here Machiavelli's earth return'd to whence it
    rose.

Subsequent stanzas also reveal the influence of the *Sepolcri*.

[1] Foscolo had developed a cult for the tombs in Santa Croce long before 1806, as may be seen in the *Ultime Lettere di Jacopo Ortis*, letter 27 Agosto. The particular patriotic treatment in the *Sepolcri*, however, is new.

45

I am afraid that too close a consideration of the *Sepolcri* will lead me, if it has not done so already, into points of detail unsuitable for this occasion. Nor would I give the impression that this highly original poem is mainly an arrangement of ideas taken from others. A poet seizes on all he requires wherever he finds it to transmute it into something new and significant. In the result we recognise great art, moved and fascinated we attempt to explore, but we do not imagine that we can explain in terms of reason what we have felt intuitively. The only excuse for historical or critical notes appended to poetry is that they are designed, within their obvious limitations, to help us to appreciate it better. The *Sepolcri* needs no testimonials and I have not set out to praise it, nor have I attempted to examine its philosophy, although this is a very possible approach and of special interest for a people that has erected a memorial on every village green and created a solemn national ritual of annual remembrance. I would rather conclude by indicating a broader aspect of romanticism revealed in the poem. The *Sepolcri* was written at a time when French power in Italy was absolute. The national consciousness, already developing in the eighteenth century, was quickened by the shock of French liberal ideas and offended by the circumstances of French domination. The effete classicism of the prevailing fashion of poetry was more suited to arcadian themes than to the expression of the still uncertain, but none the less profound, stirring of a people. The *Sepolcri*, which to a foreigner may first appeal as a work of philosophy and imagination, immediately struck Italians as the trumpet voice of national ideals. The *risorgimento* was a work of moral no less than of political renewal, and these solemn verses speaking in unmistakable sincerity of love, family, death and glory proved the inspiration of the later generations who made Italy. It is indicative of far more than a personal

47

devotion that Foscolo has given such prominence to Parini and Alfieri, the two prophets of the coming regeneration. The poet's indignation against what he considered an unjust foreign decree (vv. 51–53), the hint of dislike for ecclesiastical superstition (vv. 104–114), the bitter words directed against the selfish ruling classes (vv. 142–145), the apotheosis of the great men of the past whose memory is the only comfort left to Italy:

> *da che le mal vietate Alpi e l' alterna*
> *onnipotenza delle umane sorti*
> *armi e sostanze t' invadeano ed are*
> *e patria e, tranne la memoria, tutto.*

All these motifs were of immediate appeal to the men of the *risorgimento*. Even the scenes of classical antiquity suggested to Italians their own Roman past and they could recognise in the Trojans the mythical ancestors of Rome.

The romantic movement in Italy was above all else the symptom of a patriotism searching for freer expression, and in this

48

sense at least the *Sepolcri* belongs to that movement. A new enthusiasm, far from denying, here sanctifies tradition. Italian poetry returns to life and reality to express the inmost heart of an awakening nation.

The appeal made by the *Sepolcri* during the *risorgimento* may be illustrated in many ways, but I will restrict myself to one example. On the night of the 13th of July, 1860, some footsore Garibaldian volunteers were making their way along a track in Sicily. They were tired and hungry, in no mood for the songs that help soldiers to march. One of them, a student of law from Pavia, began to declaim the solemn verses of the *Sepolcri*. The fact has been recorded in simple words by a fellow soldier who never forgot the effect created by that poetry rising from the column of men marching through the night. He uses the words *cibo leonino*, lions' food.[1]

The great periods of Italian art and

[1] G. C. Abba, *Da Quarto al Volturno*, Vallecchi, 1925, p. 106.

letters come earlier in history, as all are aware, but I have wished to call attention to the *Sepolcri* not least as an example of Italian genius from more modern times. English sympathy for Italy is deep-rooted and genuine but, today, when we are experiencing a period of mutual misunderstanding, it is incumbent on us to pay more attention to modern Italy.

I conceive it no part of a teacher's business to enter the field of politics, still less the politics of a foreign country, but it is his business to study those deeper springs of national feeling which are often better understood in the verse of poets than in the actions of politicians. I read into the present unhappy crisis not a threat to Italian studies in this country but an incentive to study more.

Dei Sepolcri

UGO FOSCOLO

CARME A IPPOLITO PINDEMONTE

All' ombra de' cipressi e dentro l' urne
confortate di pianto è forse il sonno
della morte men duro? Ove più il sole
per me alla terra non fecondi questa
bella d' erbe famiglia e d' animali,   5
e quando vaghe di lusinghe innanzi
a me non danzeran l' ore future,
nè da te, dolce amico, udrò più il verso
e la mesta armonia che lo governa,
nè più nel cor mi parlerà lo spirto   10
delle vergini Muse e dell' Amore,
unico spirto a mia vita raminga,
qual fia ristoro a' dì perduti un sasso
che distingua le mie dalle infinite
ossa che in terra e in mar semina morte?   15
Vero è ben, Pindemonte! Anche la Speme,
ultima Dea, fugge i sepolcri; e involve
tutte cose l' obblío nella sua notte;
e una forza operosa le affatica
di moto in moto; e l' uomo e le sue tombe   20
e l' estreme sembianze e le reliquie
della terra e del ciel traveste il tempo.
Ma perchè pria del tempo a sè il mortale
invidierà l' illusïon che spento
pur lo sofferma al limitar di Dite?   25

Non vive ei forse anche sotterra, quando
gli sarà muta l' armonia del giorno,
se può destarla con soavi cure
nella mente de' suoi? Celeste è questa
corrispondenza d' amorosi sensi,   30
celeste dote è negli umani; e spesso
per lei si vive con l' amico estinto
e l' estinto con noi, se pia la terra
che lo raccolse infante e lo nutriva,
nel suo grembo materno ultimo asilo   35
porgendo, sacre le reliquie renda
dall' insultar de' nembi e dal profano
piede del vulgo, e serbi un sasso il nome,
e di fiori odorata arbore amica
le ceneri di molli ombre consoli.   40
Sol chi non lascia eredità d' affetti
poca gioia ha dell' urna; e se pur mira
dopo l' esequie, errar vede il suo spirto
fra 'l compianto de' templi acherontei,
o ricovrarsi sotto le grandi ale   45
del perdono d' Iddio; ma la sua polve
lascia alle ortiche di deserta gleba
ove nè donna innamorata preghi,
nè passeggier solingo oda il sospiro
che dal tumulo a noi manda Natura.   50
Pur nuova legge impone oggi i sepolcri
fuor de' guardi pietosi, e il nome a' morti
contende. E senza tomba giace il tuo
sacerdote, o Talia, che a te cantando

nel suo povero tetto educò un lauro   55
con lungo amore, e t' appendea corone;
e tu gli ornavi del tuo riso i canti
che il lombardo pungean Sardanapalo,
cui solo è dolce il muggito de' buoi
che dagli antri abduàni e dal Ticino   60
lo fan d' ozî beato e di vivande.
O bella Musa, ove sei tu? Non sento
spirar l' ambrosia, indizio del tuo nume,
fra queste piante ov' io siedo e sospiro
il mio tetto materno. E tu venivi   65
e sorridevi a lui sotto quel tiglio
ch' or con dimesse frondi va fremendo,
perchè non copre, o Dea, l' urna del vecchio
cui già di calma era cortese e d' ombre.
Forse tu fra' plebei tumuli guardi,   70
vagolando, ove dorma il sacro capo
del tuo Parini? A lui non ombre pose
tra le sue mura la città, lasciva
d' evirati cantori allettatrice,
non pietra, non parola; e forse l' ossa   75
col mozzo capo gl' insanguina il ladro
che lasciò sul patibolo i delitti.
Senti raspar fra le macerie e i bronchi
la derelitta cagna ramingando
su le fosse, e famelica ululando;   80
e uscir del teschio, ove fuggía la luna,
l' úpupa, e svolazzar su per le croci
sparse per la funerea campagna,

e l' immonda accusar col luttuoso
singulto i rai di che son pie le stelle   85
alle obbliate sepolture. Indarno
sul tuo poeta, o Dea, preghi rugiade
dalla squallida notte. Ah! su gli estinti
non sorge fiore, ove non sia d' umane
lodi onorato e d' amoroso pianto.   90
Dal dì che nozze e tribunali ed are
    dier alle umane belve esser pietose
    di sè stesse e d' altrui, toglieano i vivi
    all' etere maligno ed alle fere
    i miserandi avanzi che Natura   95
    con veci eterne a sensi altri destina.
    Testimonianza a' fasti eran le tombe,
    ed are a' figli; e uscían quindi i responsi
    de' domestici Lari, e fu temuto
    su la polve degli avi il giuramento: 100
    religïon che con diversi riti
    le virtù patrie e la pietà congiunta
    tradussero per lungo ordine d' anni.
    Non sempre i sassi sepolcrali a' templi
    fean pavimento; nè agl' incensi avvolto   105
    de' cadaveri il lezzo i supplicanti
    contaminò; nè le città fur meste
    d' effigïati scheletri: le madri
    balzan ne' sonni esterrefatte, e tendono
    nude le braccia su l' amato capo   110
    del lor caro lattante onde nol desti
    il gemer lungo di persona morta

chiedente la venal prece agli eredi
dal santuario. Ma cipressi e cedri,
di puri effluvî i zefiri impregnando, 115
perenne verde protendean su l' urne
per memoria perenne, e prezïosi
vasi accogliean le lacrime votive.
Rapían gli amici una favilla al sole
a illuminar la sotterranea notte 120
perchè gli occhi dell' uom cercan morendo
il sole; e tutti l' ultimo sospiro
mandano i petti alla fuggente luce.
Le fontane versando acque lustrali
amaranti educavano e vïole 125
su la funebre zolla; e chi sedea
a libar latte e a raccontar sue pene
ai cari estinti, una fragranza intorno
sentía qual d' aura de' beati Elisi.
Pietosa insania che fa cari gli orti 130
de' suburbani avelli alle britanne
vergini, dove le conduce amore
della perduta madre, ove clementi
pregaro i Genî del ritorno al prode
che tronca fe' la trïonfata nave 135
del maggior pino, e si scavò la bara.
Ma ove dorme il furor d' inclite geste
e sien ministri al vivere civile
l' opulenza e il tremore, inutil pompa
e inaugurate immagini dell' Orco 140
sorgon cippi e marmorei monumenti.

Già il dotto e il ricco ed il patrizio vulgo,
decoro e mente al bello italo regno,
nelle adulate reggie ha sepoltura
già vivo, e i stemmi unica laude. A noi   145
morte apparecchi riposato albergo,
ove una volta la fortuna cessi
dalle vendette, e l' amistà raccolga
non di tesori eredità, ma caldi
sensi e di liberal carme l' esempio.   150
A egregie cose il forte animo accendono
l' urne de' forti, o Pindemonte; e bella
e santa fanno al peregrin la terra
che le ricetta. Io quando il monumento
vidi ove posa il corpo di quel grande,   155
che temprando lo scettro a' regnatori
gli allòr ne sfronda, ed alle genti svela
di che lagrime grondi e di che sangue;
e l' arca di colui che nuovo Olimpo
alzò in Roma a' celesti; e di chi vide   160
sotto l' etereo padiglion rotarsi
più mondi, e il sole irradïarli immoto,
onde all'Anglo che tanta ala vi stese
sgombrò primo le vie del firmamento;
"Te beata, gridai, per le felici   165
aure pregne di vita, e pe' lavacri
che da' suoi gioghi a te versa Apennino.
Lieta dell' aer tuo veste la luna
di luce limpidissima i tuoi colli
per vendemmia festanti, e le convalli   170

popolate di case e d' oliveti
mille di fiori al ciel mandano incensi:
e tu prima, Firenze, udivi il carme
che allegrò l' ira al ghibellin fuggiasco,
e tu i cari parenti e l' idïoma   175
desti a quel dolce di Calliope labbro
che Amore in Grecia nudo e nudo in Roma
d' un velo candidissimo adornando,
rendea nel grembo a Venere celeste:
ma più beata chè in un tempio accolte   180
serbi l' itale glorie, uniche forse
da che le mal vietate Alpi e l' alterna
onnipotenza delle umane sorti
armi e sostanze t' invadeano ed are
e patria e, tranne la memoria, tutto.   185
Che ove speme di gloria agli animosi
intelletti rifulga ed all' Italia,
quindi trarrem gli auspicî." E a questi marmi
venne spesso Vittorio ad ispirarsi.
Irato a' patri Numi, errava muto   190
ove Arno è più deserto, i campi e il cielo
desïoso mirando; e poi che nullo
vivente aspetto gli molcea la cura,
qui posava l' austero; e avea sul volto
il pallor della morte e la speranza.   195
Con questi grandi abita eterno: e l' ossa
fremono amor di patria. Ah sì! da quella
religïosa pace un Nume parla:
e nutría contro a' Persi in Maratona

ove Atene sacrò tombe a' suoi prodi,   200
la virtù greca e l' ira. Il navigante
che veleggiò quel mar sotto l' Eubea,
vedea per l' ampia oscurità scintille
balenar d' elmi e di cozzanti brandi,
fumar le pire igneo vapor, corrusche   205
d' armi ferree vedea larve guerriere
cercar la pugna; e all' orror de' notturni
silenzi si spandea lungo ne' campi
di falangi un tumulto, e un suon di tube,
e un incalzar di cavalli accorrenti   210
scalpitanti su gli elmi a' moribondi,
e pianto, ed inni, e delle Parche il canto.
Felice te che il regno ampio de' venti,
Ippolito, a' tuoi verdi anni correvi!
E se il piloto ti drizzò l' antenna   215
oltre l' isole egèe, d' antichi fatti
certo udisti suonar dell' Ellesponto
i liti, e la marea mugghiar portando
alle prode retèe l' armi d'Achille
sovra l' ossa d'Aiace; a' generosi   220
giusta di glorie dispensiera è morte;
nè senno astuto, nè favor di regi
all' Itaco le spoglie ardue serbava,
chè alla poppa raminga le ritolse
l' onda incitata dagl' inferni Dei.   225
E me che i tempi ed il desío d' onore
fan per diversa gente ir fuggitivo,
me ad evocar gli eroi chiamin le Muse

del mortale pensiero animatrici.
Siedon custodi de' sepolcri, e quando   230
il tempo con sue fredde ale vi spazza
fin le rovine, le Pimplèe fan lieti
di lor canto i deserti, e l' armonia
vince di mille secoli il silenzio.
Ed oggi nella Troade inseminata   235
eterno splende a' peregrini un loco
eterno per la Ninfa a cui fu sposo
Giove, ed a Giove diè Dardano figlio,
onde fur Troia e Assàraco e i cinquanta
talami e il regno della giulia gente.   240
Però che quando Elettra udì la Parca
che lei dalle vitali aure del giorno
chiamava a' cori dell' Eliso, a Giove
mandò il vóto supremo, e: "Se", diceva,
"a te fur care le mie chiome e il viso   245
e le dolci vigilie, e non mi assente
premio miglior la volontà de' fati,
la morta amica almen guarda dal cielo,
onde d' Elettra tua resti la fama."
Così orando moriva. E ne gemea   250
l' Olimpio; e l' immortal capo accennando
piovea dai crini ambrosia su la Ninfa,
e fe' sacro quel corpo e la sua tomba.
Ivi posò Erittonio, e dorme il giusto
cenere d' Ilo; ivi l' iliache donne   255
sciogliean le chiome, indarno ahi! deprecando
da' lor mariti l' imminente fato;

ivi Cassandra, allor che il Nume in petto
le fea parlar di Troia il dì mortale,
venne; e all' ombre cantò carme amoroso, 260
e guidava i nepoti, e l' amoroso
apprendeva lamento ai giovinetti.
E dicea sospirando: "Oh, se mai d' Argo,
ove al Tidíde e di Laerte al figlio
pascerete i cavalli, a voi permetta   265
ritorno il cielo, invan la patria vostra
cercherete! Le mura, opra di Febo,
sotto le lor reliquie fumeranno.
Ma i Penati di Troia avranno stanza
in queste tombe; chè de' Numi è dono   270
servar nelle miserie altero nome.
E voi, palme e cipressi, che le nuore
piantan di Priamo, e crescerete ahi presto!
di vedovili lagrime innaffiati,
proteggete i miei padri: e chi la scure   275
asterrà pio dalle devote frondi,
men si dorrà di consanguinei lutti
e santamente toccherà l' altare.
Proteggete i miei padri. Un dì vedrete
mendico un cieco errar sotto le vostre   280
antichissime ombre, e brancolando
penetrar negli avelli, e abbracciar l' urne,
e interrogarle. Gemeranno gli antri
secreti, e tutta narrerà la tomba
Ilio raso due volte e due risorto   285
splendidamente su le mute vie

per far più bello l' ultimo trofeo
ai fatati Pelidi. Il sacro vate,
placando quelle afflitte alme col canto,
i prenci argivi eternerà per quante   290
abbraccia terre il gran padre Oceàno.
E tu onore di pianti, Ettore, avrai
ove fia santo e lagrimato il sangue
per la patria versato, e finchè il sole
risplenderà su le sciagure umane."   295

www.ingramcontent.com/pod-product-compliance
Ingram Content Group UK Ltd.
Pitfield, Milton Keynes, MK11 3LW, UK
UKHW042140280225
455719UK00001B/1